Pebbles
and
Pods

A Book of Nature Crafts

By Goldie Taub Chernoff

Pictures by Margaret Hartelius

SCHOLASTIC INC.
New York Toronto London Auckland Sydney

Have you ever collected stones or shells? Have you ever gathered leaves in the fall? Do you know you can make beautiful prints with weeds? Or that paintings can be made with sand? This book will show you how to make all sorts of things with materials you can find outside. There are many interesting objects you can collect without hurting the environment. Look for them the next time you go out. Look on the ground, in yards, under trees, near fences, near bushes, in the park and at the beach. If you look carefully, you will see many things you never noticed before.

ISBN 0-590-40295-1

12 11 10 9 8 7 6 5 4 3 2 1   6 7 8 9/8 0 1/9

Printed in the U.S.A.

CONTENTS

Spatter Prints

You will need an old toothbrush, a sheet of paper, paint, cardboard, ferns, twigs, leaves, straight pins, and a stick or a piece of window screen.

- Place the sheet of paper on the cardboard.

- Arrange the leaves, ferns, twigs on the paper any way you wish.

- Stick pins in to hold the nature materials in place on the cardboard.

- Dip the toothbrush in the paint. Shake off any extra paint.

- Hold the toothbrush a few inches above the paper, bristle side down.

- Scrape the bristles of the toothbrush toward you with a stick. (If you scrape away from you, the spray will spatter you.) For another way to make a spray, hold a piece of screen or a tea strainer a few inches above the paper. Rub the toothbrush over the screen.

- Remove the pins and the nature materials and hang your picture up.

Wood and Leaf Rubbings

- Place a sheet of paper over a flat piece of wood.

- Rub the broad side of a pencil point or crayon back and forth over the paper.

- The lines and bumps in the grain of the wood will show up clearly and make a design.

You can also make a tree or a telephone-pole rubbing. Tape a sheet of paper to the tree or telephone pole and rub the paper with pencil or crayon.

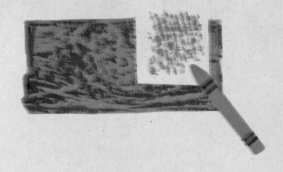

- For leaf rubbings, place a leaf with the veins up between a fold of white paper. Rub the paper with a pencil or crayon and the design will show up.

Try making rubbings with stones, shells, and other objects you find.

Wood, Leaf, and Shell Prints

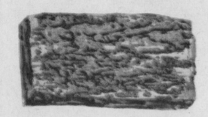

Use a piece of wood from the beach, park, woods, carpenter shop, or lumberyard. The rougher the wood is, the better your design will be.

• Brush paint over the surface of the wood.

• While the paint is wet, press the wood down hard on a sheet of paper.

• Turn the wood to another position and press again.

You can print the same way with leaves, seed pods, weeds, flat sea shells (clam, oyster, scallop).

Sand Painting

We learned to do sand painting from the Indians of the West
who used them in many ceremonies. Here's how you
can make your own beautiful sand paintings.

You will need:
a pail or coffee can of sand
liquid food coloring
several cans or jars with tops for
coloring and storing sand

newspaper
large sheets of heavy paper
white glue in a squeeze bottle

Your sand painting can be two or three or
many colors. Mix each color separately.

Now you are ready to make a design:

- Put a small amount of sand in a screw-
  top jar or can.

- Add liquid food coloring a few drops at
  a time. The more food coloring you add,
  the darker the sand will be.

- Cover the jar and shake.

- Spread each mixture out on separate sheets
  of newspaper to dry.

- After the sand has dried, pour each color
  into its own container.

- First, draw the design on a large sheet
  of paper.

- Spread the paper on the ground.

- Squeeze white glue over the design. Do
  a small section at a time.

- Dribble colored sand over the wet glue
  with your fingers.

- Continue to glue and sand the design in small
  sections until the sand painting is complete.

- When the glue is dry, shake off any loose sand.

See-Through Decoration

• Over a sheet of brown paper place a sheet of wax paper.

• Arrange a few leaves or ferns on the wax paper.

• Scrape crayon shavings over the leaves.

• Place a second sheet of wax paper on top.

• Cover this with another sheet of brown paper.

• Slide a warm iron slowly over the brown paper. The crayon and wax paper will melt and seal your leaf design inside.

• The See-Through is ready to hang.

Shadow Box

Find a box that is fairly shallow — such as a handkerchief box, a tie box, or the cover of a shoe box.

• Paint the box and let it dry.

• Place a group of outdoor objects on the bottom of the box to make a design.

• Lift each object carefully. Put a little glue on the bottom and gently press the object back into place.

• Allow the glue to dry. Hang the shadow box up.

Mosaics

- Take the cover of a cottage cheese or margarine container.
- Place one or two shells or acorn cups at the center of the cover and glue them in place.
- Working from the center to the outside edge, fill in the rest of your design by gluing on watermelon seeds, colored pebbles, gravel, beads, macaroni, pieces of foil, or other small objects.

For a Simpler Method

- Roll clay flat and spread it about half an inch thick inside a deep paper plate or foil tray.
- On the clay arrange stones, pebbles, twigs, shells, seeds, etc., to form a design.
- Press the nature materials down a little into the clay.

Stone Figures

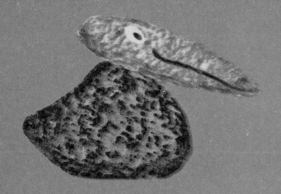

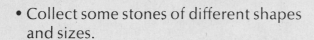

- Collect some stones of different shapes and sizes.

- Choose one of the larger stones for the body of your figure.

- Smaller stones can be added for eyes, head, arms, and so on.

- Join the stones together with bits of cotton soaked in liquid white glue.

- Allow each part of the figure to dry before adding a new part.

- Small details may be painted on.

Nature Creatures

- Start with a base of clay, soap, or styrofoam to keep your sculpture from falling over.

- Work from the bottom up using milkweed pods, acorns, or pine cones.

- Fasten each part that is added with glue or glue-soaked bits of cotton.

Apple Head Goblins

- Peel a medium-sized apple.

- With your fingers press in eyes, nose, and mouth.

- Allow the apple to dry in a cool, dry place
  for about two weeks until it is brown and small.

- Poke a stick into the bottom of the apple.

- To make the dress: Fold three pieces of
  tissue paper or cornhusks in half, as shown.
  Make a little hole in the middle. Slide
  the tissues or cornhusks onto the stick.

- To make arms: Roll up two or three pieces
  of tissue paper or cornhusks and tie the ends.

- Slip the arms up underneath the dress.
  Tie the dress at the waist so the arms
  stay in place.

- Spread the skirt out. Add hair and a hat
  or other decorations.

Bird Feeders

1. • Make four holes at opposite sides of a cardboard or plastic container. (Use containers from cheese, margarine, yogurt, and so on.)

   • Tie strings through the holes for a handle as shown.

   • Fill the container with small pieces of apple, nuts, and/or beef suet.

   • Hang the bird feeder on a branch or place it on an outside windowsill or porch.

2. • Cut out the four sides of a half-gallon milk container as shown.

   • Poke two holes through the top of the container.

   • Tie a long string through each hole.

   • Fill the bird feeder with food and hang it outside.

3. • Spread peanut butter all over a large pine cone.

   • Hang it on a string outside your window where you can watch the birds feed.

Mystery Nuts

- Fill one half of a walnut shell with a painted pebble, a tiny sea shell, a piece of candy or a folded note with a secret message on it.

- Glue the second half in place or seal with tape. You can also use two acorn cups.

- Tie with a ribbon.

- Use as party favors, get-well presents, birthday wishes, or ornaments for a "Friendship Tree."

God's Eyes

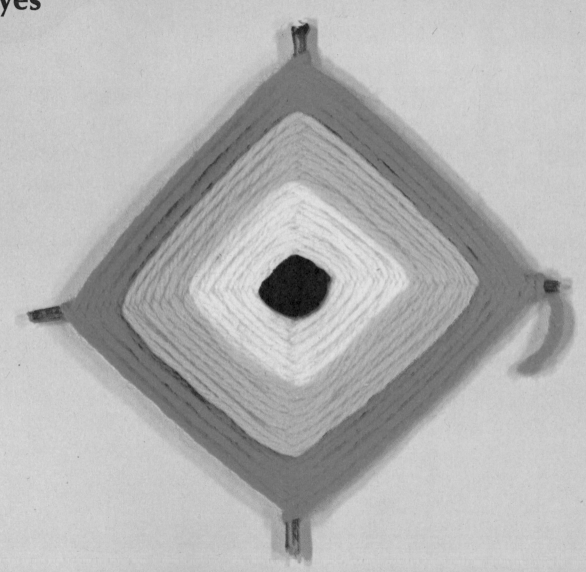

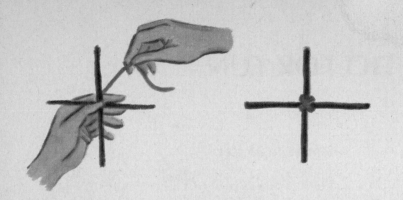

- Make a cross with two twigs or sticks and tie them together at the center with colored yarn.

- Working from the center, loop the yarn around one arm of the cross.

- Going in the same direction, loop the yarn around each arm in turn. Keep the yarn tight. As each row is completed, push the yarn down toward the center.

- Poke the tail ends into the completed rows so the knot won't show.

- Add new pieces of yarn in different colors as you go. Simply knot onto the ends of the old pieces.

- When the arms are all filled with yarn, end off by tying the yarn to one of the arms.

- Glue or hang acorn cups or seed pods to the ends of the arms if you wish. Hang as a decoration.

MORE THINGS TO DO FOR FUN

Shadow Pictures

Go outside and find a sharp shadow that is made by a tree, a bush, flowers, a fence, a baby carriage or a bicycle. Morning or late afternoon when the shadows are longest is the best time to find a sharp shadow. Spread a large sheet of paper on the ground so that the shadow falls on it. Paint, chalk, or crayon all around the shadow. Move the paper a little and draw around the new shadow. If you wish, the spaces can be filled in with color.

Cloud Pictures

Look at the shapes of clouds. Draw a picture of clouds with chalk, crayon, paint, or felt pen. Glue your cloud-picture inside a decorated box lid and hang up.

Stones in Water

Place a collection of clean stones in a jar of water. Add a few drops of liquid bleach to keep the water fresh. Place the jar in the sun. What colors do you see?

A Game to Play

Put a nature collection in a large paper bag or box. With eyes closed, each player gently feels an object inside and tries to guess what it is. The object is then pulled out. If a player has guessed right he or she gets a star. Keep passing the bag or box around until all the objects have been pulled from the bag. The player with the most stars gets a Mystery Nut or other prize.